SECOND ACT WRITINGS

Volume 2

Poems on Life, Love, & Other Musings

R.H.W. DORSEY

SECOND ACTS PRESS

Copyright © 2019 R.H.W. Dorsey

All rights reserved.

No part of this publication may be reproduced, distributed, or transmitted in any form or by any means, including photocopying, internet usage, recording, or other electronic mechanical methods, without the prior written permission of the author, except in the case of brief quotations embodied in critical reviews and certain other noncommercial uses permitted by copyright law.

Printed in the United States of America

First paperback edition July 2019

ISBN 978-1-7332702-2-9

Second Acts Press

www.secondactspress.com

Front cover art by R.H.W. Dorsey

Acknowledgments

My heartfelt thanks to Sage Cohen whose course *Write a Poem a Day* in April 2019, inspired many poems in this collection.

To the reader,

The poems in this book were written during a time of healing and personal reflection. The prompted material in the above-mentioned course inspired many of the words on the following pages. Other poems included here were inspired by my love of the creative process.

Included in this collection are poems that employ various poetic devices and poetic forms. Thanks for accompanying me on a continuing journey toward finding my true poetic voice. I invite you to look past the surface to find a deeper meaning of your own understanding.

Dedication

To my granddaughters who fill my life with love, laughter, and hope. I love you all.

Forever, Nana.

Contents

LIFE 1
My Sun 2
Talking to my Sister 3
Healers Disguised as Children 4
Solace 5
Mourning Morning 6
For my Granddaughters 7
Sweet Time 8
Collectors of Dust 9
Dear Transplant Recipient, ... 10
Fineness Personified 11
Lessons 12
You're Enough 13
I Did 14
Peace at Dusk 15
Here for the Duration 16
LOVE 17
Soul's Beauty 18
Waking to You 19
The Seeker 20
Predestined Us 21

Cinquain Love	22
Acrostic Flashbacks	23
Heart's Song Revealed	24
Anticipating Forever	25
One Two, One Two	26
Child of Venus	27
OTHER MUSINGS	28
Jealous of Edgy	29
Succinctly	30
Not a White Elephant	31
Briefcase	32
All Star Chuck Taylor Rant	33
Cascade of Jealousy	34
Glories in the Morning	35
Pondering	37
Pen Musings	38
A Daydream Prose	39
Serenity of Noise	40
Perpetual Journey	41
Early Broadcast	42
Parks and Rec Summer of Sixteen	43
Freedom Territory	45
Console in Need of Consoling	46
Electric Strumming Dreams	47

LIFE

My Sun

I saw the sun shining
through my room darkening
curtains on a morning of
sadness and depression. I
heard the sun say, "Get up
you've lived to see another
day." The voice in my head
may have been God, or maybe
God sent the sun to talk to me.
I was getting a do-over that day.

The feeling of renewal and second chances
are gifts my sun gives me every day. As a
child, I heard the family say, "Let's
thank God for allowing us to see the
sunshine another day." Maybe I'm
drawn to the sun because of
those affirmations given
to me so long ago. Days
of overcast skies don't
give me pause. My sun
never leaves.

Talking to My Sister

I talked to her spirit last
night and told her about the poem
I wrote on how she helped me with
my boots in that classroom when
we were children. She said that's
nice honey, did it make you sad

to remember? What really made me sad
was thinking about you not being here,
I said. She said please don't be sad,
I had to leave, there was so much pain
but it's gone now. I'm sorry you had
to endure the pain for so long,

I said. I want to write more about you
so that you won't be forgotten. Whatever
you decide, it's ok honey, she said.
Then she said, I know you won't forget me.

Healers Disguised as Children

Sunbeams of love
run around my house
wonderfully polluting
the air with squeals of
laughter and joy.

Gloriously, they play
unaware of their healing
powers. I drink in the soothing
elixir of their presence.

Solace

Born from a woman
with a lion's spirit
and a heart of gold,
I go about the business
of living every day
to walk on soft carpets
at dawn still groggy
from sleep, but on rare
occasions my feet seem to
flow like a stingray
traveling through ocean waters.
The yellow and teal designs
on my teapot are reminders
of beauty in the world.
Cold faucet water pouring
into the pot sounds like
tiny waterfalls on metal.
The tall, wood-stained barrier
with noisy hinges threaten
to act as a harbinger of
my arrival like the wolf's howl
to its pack. My wooden door
Is a fortress of seclusion
and its lock is my first love
at the beginning of each day.

Mourning Morning

I contemplate the result of
staying prone in my safe place.
Solitude is what I crave while the
morning sun makes its intrusive entrance
across moist eyelids too tired to open.

I wanted the night to last forever
and remain in a forgetful sleep
away from the realities of life
and sorrow. How do I reconcile
with a mind that objects to facts?

Your departure was ill-timed and quick.
With a heart too fragile to feel,
I stay surrounded by warm quilts
that hide my endless tears but not my pain.
I live for the night and sleep that forgets.

For My Granddaughters

Your feelings of being misunderstood
and disillusioned won't always be what
makes you cry. Emotions are like waves
rushing through and around you, but
be assured they'll soon dissipate. Know
the waves will likely return throughout
your lifetime. Your everchanging path
will make certain you feel the waves and
begin to welcome them.

These present days are the days you'll
wish for some time long into the future. So,
enjoy the awkwardness this time begs. Seek
out answers to your questions and be curious
on purpose. Satisfaction should feel right and
never rationalized. Ride your waves! Your
intuition is waiting for you to take ahold of her
and triumph!

Sweet Time

Morning light returns with the
Robin's sweet song. I believe
in time.

A life ceases as a newborn's
sweet cry wakes its lungs. I
believe in time.

My Dogwood blooms with
April's sweet warmth. I believe
in time.

Impaired bodies can heal with
love and care, can't they? I believe
in time. I hope time believes in me.

Collectors of Dust

The ceramic swan from Grandma's table
with yellowed tape holding its neck together.

Mom's stone elephant sculpture with the
chipped trunk. Dad's Santa Claus figurine

collection. Auntie's vintage Samsonite hard shell
makeup box luggage. My ninth-grade English

notebook held together by three silver book rings.
The eighth-grade graduation ceremony dress with

large pink sash. The wooden phonograph/radio/tv
console from the 1960s. Fortran and Cobol mainframe

programming notebooks. The newborn ankle ID
bracelet from 1980. Hundreds of Polaroid and

Instamatic photos from the 70s and 80s. The 1990s
USAir first-class amenity kit. Milestone and memorabilia

holding little or no monetary value but too priceless
to discard.

Dear Transplant Recipient,

Two Thanksgivings have passed without her
presence which brought joy and laughter.
Her living space remains pristine and clear
to guard our memories that she was here.
We're content in knowing someone survived
as a result of a life she was deprived.
Your thoughts and prayers are appreciated,
but we hoped fate would've waited.
Our gift was unselfish and without strife.
We hope her heart brings longevity to his life.

Fineness Personified

I want to go out with all my
being, but my mind sits me down to
ponder reasons, better yet, excuses
for not showing up to moments of
life that would surely uplift my spirit.
I'm fine.

I multitask in one thousand square feet
of square space praising technology
for its handy tools that make staying in
place safe while keeping me from a reality
my brain chooses not to deal with at present.
I'm fine.

Intelligent enough to be aware anxiety and
depression are obstacles; foolish enough
to ignore the symptoms that threaten more
brokenness – I admit no quandary. My
psyche holds the answers my mind ignores.
I'm fine.

Waiting for the next tragedy to force me
out of the funk is ominous but surprisingly
effective. My best foot forward often reveals
itself at times of great upheaval and crisis.
I'm fine.

Lessons

Funeral services for those who passed on happened often in a community inhabited by people of all ages. As a child, I learned to accept the old grow weak and leave us. Death was always a scary prospect to my

young mind, but I can't count on one hand how many homegoing services saw me in attendance. It seemed a rite of passage to witness the tearful goodbyes paired with joyful singing and reminiscing. Few were

deemed too young to see dead loved ones off on their journeys as I remember. That old people die was a fact until my revelation of death can happen too soon. He was seventeen with a vibrant spirit making

him larger than life in my circle of young teen friends. The day I saw and heard him breathe his last living breath was the day the anesthetization of my feelings about death began. It was on that day I learned young

people die too. Decades passed with many homegoing services attended for both young and old. Death is no longer a boogeyman but thoughts of its reality bring twinges of fear at times. It is a sure and unwelcome acquaintance.

You're Enough

If you care to measure your life by the
present states of things, you may be
unhappy with what's revealed. Do you
know your declines are lessons in regrowth?
Believe the rock-bottoms you claim are
machinations of a self-imposed extinction.
To embrace a wallow in pity as your destiny
is to offend those who made you possible.
You must summon inner strength born of
kindred souls. You're beautiful, handsome,
unique, awesome and worthy of a blessed life.
Rise above your fears and fight for a life
filled with the hope of your ancestors.
I'm holding you. I see you. I love you.

I Did

I wanted to feel unconditional love.
I wanted to sing to an audience in Nashville, USA.
I wanted to roller skate and dance under a disco ball in the wee hours of the morning.
I wanted to make angels in the snow as an adult.
I wanted to love unselfishly.
I wanted to laugh and cry in the summer rain.
I wanted to forgive with absolute sincerity.
I wanted to have faith in a higher power.
I wanted to sing the babies to sleep with lullabies.
I wanted to visit Disneyland and Disneyworld.
I wanted to play air guitar to music during long drives in the car.
I wanted to lay my body on the grass and look up at a starry sky.
I wanted to stand near the cliffs of Niagara Falls.
I wanted to author poems and books to speak my heart and imagination.
I wanted to be by my parents' sides as they transitioned from this world.
I wanted to be a mother.

Peace at Dusk

Dusk is attempting to settle on my doorstep.
Night will surely come for a final bow enveloping
me while the moon observes my fate.

I knew mornings of youth and vitality spent
gazing at sunlight that seemed endless. Adventures
fueled my curiosity through middays.

Afternoons were my favorites. Lost innocence brought
forth life experience and offspring rewards.
Independence was scary but felt right.

Dusk can take its rightful place as my skies darken. I've
known mornings with sunshine and afternoons filled with
love. My spirit is fine with the remnants of my existence
left behind.

Here for the Duration

Still here because sadness is overrated
and given far too much attention when
joy feels better than anything you'd

imagine. Still here because I'm
egotistical enough to believe I matter
to at least a few in this world. Still

here because my spirit commands a
battle for life against a mind pushing
me into sporadic stupors. Still here

because those beautiful faces appear
in my thoughts to pull me back from
the brink of endless depression. Still

here because love sits at my side and
reminds me in my darkest hours the
light stands in wait for me.

LOVE

Soul's Beauty

Your soul's beauty
Illuminates love in
my heart like the
sunrise lights up the sky.

Waking to You

Your love never ceases
like the unwavering
sunrise. Timely and true.

As the morning dew forms
on tiny blades of grass,
I live to love again.

The Seeker

I was reckless. I
lost innocence. I

knew joy. I
felt pain. I

cried shock. I
failed often. I

I made peace. I
knew love.

Predestined Us

We met on the moon
eons before any rendezvous
of our earthly forms.

As molecules in outer
galaxies, we collided in
space initiating sparks of

energy to ensure repeat
engagements that would
ultimately serve as the

catalyst for the meeting
between our physical souls
at the appointed time.

Cinquain Love

People
sometimes find true
love in the second half
of their lives, but are they lucky?
Maybe.

Call it
kismet or just
inevitable fate;
one thing is for sure, love has found
a home.

Acrostic Flashbacks

Blooming love for you was exciting and is forever
Etched in my memories of our yesterdays.
Longing for your constant presence
On past days of solitude brought
Vivid daydreams of our next
Encounter. You remain
Devoted as ever.

Heart's Song Revealed

It's difficult to figure
out exact moments we
come into our own true selves.

My soul placed a beacon
deep inside the bowels of
my existence for a signal from you.

Melodies of longing for you
echoed in my head like a metronome
in tempo, until you were revealed in your time.

Self-validation struggles
have long since departed.
Ticking clocks threatened my demise.

The imperfect and true
self has sung the most beautiful
aria I've waited many lifetimes to hear.

Anticipating Forever

Pensive thoughts of you were often when
Awe of *us* first inhabited my mind. Our
Sensual exchanges consumed with
Soft-spoken and sexy promises
Ignited our anticipation. Love
On a pedestal waited for
New Beginnings.

One Two, One Two

One and a half were a reality for years. Then
two came with tricks to *save us*.

Two was handily removed for peace. Then
one and a half were free and content.

One accepted another two for security. Then
two came with baggage too heavy to manage.

Two was released as the half became whole. Then
one became one alone as the whole embraced its oneness.

One enjoyed boundless freedom and gained wisdom. Then a
two more unique and long-awaited appeared like a gift.

One and unique two enjoyed mutual faith and love. Then
one and two became an indivisible set called *us*.

Child of Venus

Calm infatuation invaded my heart as I gazed
Upon a beautiful face oozing with polite
Pleasantries. You offered fellowship and
Intoxicating wisdom to souls
Desperate for hope.

OTHER MUSINGS

Jealous of Edgy

Words that tout death and sorrow
are boosted by the masses as
powerful pieces of art that stand above
displays of passion and humor.

Cheerful passages void of evil and harmful
intentions get pushed aside
into the abyss and labeled trite nothings
below words of sexism and racism.

Give me words that tickle my face like
a feather falling through the air
destined for only me. Let the goosebumps
rise while my eyes dazzle.

Pen conversations that speak of happiness
as I imagine all possible meanings.
Write your thoughts as though endorphins
commanded your soul to speak to me.

Succinctly

I admire flowery
poetry and sometimes
wish I could pen elegant
phrases. But, my soul's
expressions are succinct.

Not a White Elephant

Did you know pachyderms are lucky?
At least, that's what I heard.
It now sits with pictures and knick-knacks
on our shelf of memories.

The beady red eyes and raised trunk
adds charm to her light gray statue.
Guests often question and I answer,
Did you know pachyderms are lucky?

Doubling as a paperweight at times,
it sits immovable by young hands.
Some say it keeps bad luck away.
At least, that's what I heard.

I don't believe in superstitions
but it'll stay in place until I'm gone.
I think she'd be tickled to know
it now sits with pictures and knick-knacks.

We crack a smile at the cast stone elephant
that stayed in her house for years.
It will continue to have a place
on our shelf of memories.

Briefcase

It'll be here when I'm ready
to sort through the papers
chronicling a storied life
filled with grace.

I'll bet it holds has vivid memories
as it sits patiently waiting
for inspection of its contents.
It'll be here when I'm ready.

It laughs every time I walk by.
The taunts and teases never cease
as it knows I'm not ready
to sort through the papers.

Is today going to be the day?
shouts the black sturdy briefcase.
Too busy to check the papers
chronicling a storied life?

I hold important things
and someday I'll hold yours too.
Reserve time to look at the cards
of a life filled with grace.

All Star Chuck Taylor Rant

The corner of a dark and desolate closet
became our home after serving your
purpose. Bright red replacements sealed
our fate. We bore the brunt of the impact
on hard concrete streets. We suffered as
odor from your sweaty feet permeated our
insides on countless journeys leading to your
ultimate good fortune. Why did you discard us?
We're worn and dulled in color, but
intact and still fit to serve. I speak for my twin
when I say we didn't deserve the level of disrespect
we received. As we sat atop a box of riffraff you
no longer treasure, luck smiled on us in the form
of a spirited young lady. She gave us new life by
hurling us up high away from your box of unwanted
property. We're free now. You're gone away to
pursue dreams. Our new perch provides vistas of
fine architecture and cityscapes now lost to you as
you travel from this place that was never your home.
Streetlamps illuminate our nights while sunlight
brightens our days. Fresh air is the stuff of our dreams.

Cascade of Jealousy

Resentment rears its awful head
with no regard to right or wrong.
We can ponder the reasons why

the line between good and evil
stays as thin as a piece of thread.
Resentment rears its awful head.

Perpetrators do their deeds
as they cheat and lie endlessly
with no regard of right or wrong.

Success in life through hard work
is often viewed with jealous eyes.
We can ponder the reasons why.

Glories in the Morning

I believe admirers of morning
glories are awestruck at the
welcome it gives to the sun.

Comparable to an attractive lothario,
I imagine morning glories waiting with
conceit to be adored.

Allergic to honeybees? Remove morning
glory vines that tempt pollinating
honeybees with its open petals.

The morning glory's short life is made
even shorter as the unknowing child stuffs
the buds in sticky pockets.

Purposely crushed morning glory buds
produce noises likened to tiny firecrackers
when crushed against pavements.

The morning glory recognizes its
purpose and in bloom willingly
accepts all suitors.

Oh, to be a blooming morning
glory flower filled with unabashed
acceptance of its colorful beauty.

Incoming hummingbirds seize
the opportunity of morning
glory flower's nectar.

Entwining vines crawl along
doorways producing deliberate
hues and decoration.

Why not find a morning glory vine
with ready buds and sit close in
watch before dawn? The wonder
of the bloom is breathtaking.

Colorless and closed, the morning
glory flower slowly uncoils petals to
emerging sunlight yielding the
loveliest of blooms.

We open and close our five-fingered
hands at will; while morning glories'
five petals stand at the mercy of a rising
sun.

Morning glories in bright bloom
offered a first look at nature's beauty
to a young girl wandering by the fence
after daybreak.

Pondering

Does the unborn child feel pain?
Do babies have their own language?
Are out-of-body near-death experiences real?
I'll leave those questions to the scientists
and researchers to prove or disprove.

What I'm sure of is water makes
things wet, birds fly throughout the sky,
I need oxygen to breathe, sunshine makes me
happy, I love my family, and ice cream is a
blessing and evil at the same time. I pray

because I was taught to pray as a
child and it stuck. As a child, I wondered
if my God was the correct God. The answers to
my questions are less important as the years
pass. Faith in my Creator sustains me. Do

you have questions about the mystery
of life? Do you accept everything as it is?
If we get answers to our questions, do you think
we're better for knowing the answers at the
end of our lives? Will those answers bring
value to the life we lived?

Pen Musings

I'd be hard-pressed to pinpoint a day in my adventurous beginnings when the pen decided to speak for me. In retrospect, I believe my pen got its wings in my early years of stifled expression.

The pen made its debut most likely on a day filled with melancholy. I imagine it took flight to save possible internal combustion of my young spirit. Freedom was found as the pen scribed the sights and

sounds of my youth. Today, the pen no longer commands my total expression as vocal words also enjoy freedom. The pen and I have a mutual relationship of reflection, laughter, joy, and devastation.

The pen remains my healer, confidant, and muse.

A Daydream Prose

I've never clogged myself with worries about
my sink backing up with pasta and coffee
grounds. Pasta is far too delicious
to waste in a sink's pipes and
coffee grounds make
great compost.
It is easy to be a klutz when walking on cobblestone
streets wearing stiletto
heels. The constant tiptoeing on
stones and threat of ankle
twisting is such
a drag.
If only I had a house overlooking a lake with trees and
mountains in the distance,
I would take a picture on each
of the three hundred
sixty-five days
of the year.

Serenity of Noise

The sound of rain dancing on
my roof and windows at dawn
are calming. There's something
about the noise of water that's
very Zen.

Hearing ocean waves splash
against the shore lulls me into
a restful sleep. There's something
about the noise of water that's
very Zen.

Boiling water pouring from a tea
kettle into a ceramic mug does fuel
my tranquility. There's something
about the noise of water that's
very Zen.

Water trickling from atop a fountain
into a bottom filled with coins for
wishing sounds lovely. There's something
about the noise of water that's
very Zen.

Perpetual Journey

Recycled garments unchanged in sight,
but more pleasant in their aroma
sit next to her on a seat
that absorbs vibrations
of familiar highways.
She allows the
outside wind to
tunnel through
cracked windows
providing noise to
occupy an anxious mind
on a mission. This repeated
journey to the place with bright,
and long corridors filled with scents
of chemicals that mask the pungent human
process is necessary. She enters the
room with fragile bodies aged
through time. Their faces
are diverse with sadness,
acceptance, wisdom,
patience and
possibly
hope.

Early Broadcast

Oh look, Hoda, the lights in the kitchen came on. What do you think it'll be today Kathie Lee? I'm sure it'll be something tasty and warm, Hoda. She looks kind of groggy, so we may see the caffeine flow today. Kath,

I'm thinking she'll head to the coffee maker, or maybe go the instant route and nuke it. Well, I can tell you one thing Hoda, she seems like she needs a pick me up. Oh, you folks know I mean that in the nicest way! Yes, Kath,

we know you do. Wait, it looks as though she's heading for the lower cabinet. Oh, and she went old school! A tea kettle? Hoda, I haven't seen that done in years. I guess it's still a thing. Now, the water's almost boiling. I wonder what

type of tea bag she'll go for this morning, Kath? Her favorite orange spice or Earl Grey? Well, whatever it is, it'll be hot. Can you believe it Hoda? She's reaching for an infuser. Oh look, that's a cute purple one, Kathie Lee. She's going for

the loose-leaf Mango Peach. Sounds good, huh? Yes, it does. I wonder if there's a wine in Mango Peach? Wow, it's a whistling tea kettle. I had one of those years ago. Who has time now, am I right, Hoda? I know what you mean Kath,

I get mine at the shop down on the corner. We live in a fast-paced world, Hoda, and don't I know it. I see she's pouring the water into her clear glass mug. It looks kind of cool with the infuser, doesn't it Kathie Lee? Yep, it does,

Hoda. I know the infuser thingy will take a bit of time. Stay with us folks, we'll be right back after this message from our sponsors.

Parks and Rec Summer of Sixteen

Those sturdy white trucks with dark
blue lettering rolled out of the garage
after dawn transporting crews and tools

to my city's streets. Hot summer days
were when those workers earned
pay in endurance, sweat, and strength.

I was along for the ride as a teen seeking
summer wages. My peers and I sat with
the regular crew in the back of a large

pickup truck. We traveled daily on assigned
routes with the purpose of beautifying the
neighborhoods. I saw tall grass in untended

empty lots, weeds sprouting from cracks in
cement sidewalks and debris that lined the
bottom of curbs for miles. We were

provided with trimmers and shears to remove
sprawling weeds threatening driver's
views on narrow winding streets. Workers

wielded large industrial brooms to sweep
and remove dirt, pebbles, and trash down
city blocks temporarily improving the

streets' décor. The heat of the sun during that
summer never failed to call out beads of
perspiration from my pores long before the day

was done. Lunchtime was a short and welcome respite. The work was physical and character building. My sweaty skin was both disgusting and

satisfying as I arrived home each day feeling accomplished. My damp clothes at the day's end were badges for the hardest work I've ever done.

Freedom Territory

Our territory is our freedom. We
roam play and hunt to survive.
We arrived on these lands long
before your kind invaded our habitat.

Your world is your freedom. You
remain both strange and familiar as
you give and withhold sustenance. Your
false sense of security will be your downfall.

Our territory is our freedom. We
don't fear your presence or your
attention as we accept your offerings.
You are the food givers.

Your world is your freedom. You
admire our mysterious aura that
summons your return to feed curious
minds. We are the food-takers.

Our territory is our freedom. We
survive on the meat of the land as
required. Both wild and tame, we stay
enigmas to your inquisitive minds.

Your world is your freedom. You
fail to grasp we are creatures of the
environment. You and your young
will always be our prey.

Console in Need of Consoling

The old console sings the blues or at
least it did ages ago before I was grown.
It slept in a living room that doubled as
a bedroom for two. The vinyl records it
played throughout the day still echo in
my head at times. Its radio programs

ignited my vivid imagination as a child.
I spent special parts of my day with Mr.
Rogers talking to me from the picture
tube. I imagine if the console were human
it would wear comfortable shoes and eat
eggs with toast for breakfast back then.

I imagine it wants to know why its demise
is confinement to a cold, dusty and dark
storage when its turntable played Aretha,
Mahalia and Marvin. It showed us the moon
landing in '69 as our eyes were fixed in
absolute wonder at history unfolding. The

radio reports of MLK's fatal departure from
this life blasted through its speakers that
April day in '68. The old console can no longer
spin records televise or broadcast. Its wooden
frame and sturdy legs have stood time's test.
I selfishly keep it hostage for memory's sake.

Electric Strumming Dreams

Familiar drumbeats are quick
to perk my senses as my
mind alerts me of what
will surely cause my head to

move up and down and side to side.
Sounds of amplified chords begin
abruptly as if the electric
guitar's strings were strummed

before the drum intro. The
guitar solo stands for itself
with no real need for any
accompanying lyrics.

Chords must be learned before
any last breaths stake their claim.
I want to feel the strings vibrate
as I pick to my heart's content.

To create and witness sounds
sending my heart and mind
on thought journeys lasting beyond
the music is my mission.

www.ingramcontent.com/pod-product-compliance
Lightning Source LLC
Chambersburg PA
CBHW060343080526
44584CB00013B/905